Read-About® Science

Will It Float or Sink?

By Melissa Stewart

Subject Consultant
Andrew Fraknoi
Chair, Astronomy Program
Foothill College
Los Altos Hills, California

Reading Consultant
Cecilia Minden-Cupp, PhD
Former Director of the Language and Literacy Program
Harvard Graduate School of Education
Cambridge, Massachusetts

Children's Press®
A Division of Scholastic Inc.
New York   Toronto   London   Auckland   Sydney
Mexico City   New Delhi   Hong Kong
Danbury, Connecticut

12/11
CL G

Designer: Herman Adler Design
Photo Researcher: Caroline Anderson
The photo on the cover shows children in a rowboat.

Library of Congress Cataloging-in-Publication Data

Stewart, Melissa.
  Will it float or sink? / by Melissa Stewart; consultants, Andrew Fraknoi,
Cecilia Minden-Cupp.
      p. cm. — (Rookie Read-About Science)
  Includes index.
  ISBN 0-516-24955-X (lib. bdg.)   0-516-23737-3 (pbk.)
  1. Floating bodies—Juvenile literature. 2. Buoyant ascent
(Hydrodynamics)—Juvenile literature. I. Title. II. Series.
  QC147.5.S74 2006
  532'.25—dc22   2005021755

CHILDREN'S PRESS, and ROOKIE READ-ABOUT®,
and associated logos are trademarks and/or registered trademarks
of Scholastic Library Publishing. SCHOLASTIC and associated logos
are trademarks and/or registered trademarks of Scholastic Inc.

1 2 3 4 5 6 7 8 9 10 R 15 14 13 12 11 10 09 08 07 06

A boat can float in
the water.

So can a plastic spoon.
But a metal spoon sinks.

A plastic spoon and a
metal spoon are made
of matter.

So are a Ping-Pong ball
and a golf ball. Everything
in the world is made
of matter.

A Ping-Pong ball and a golf ball are about the same size. But a Ping-Pong ball is much lighter than a golf ball. That is because it has less matter in the same amount of space.

The Ping-Pong ball is also lighter than water. That's why it floats.

The golf ball is heavier than water. That's why it sinks.

Ping-Pong balls are full of air. So are soccer balls and beach balls.

Why can things that are full of air float? Because air is so light.

A metal spoon sinks. But a large metal pot floats.

Why can a metal pot float? Because it is full of air.

When an object is put into a liquid, the object pushes against the liquid. The liquid pushes back.

If the object is lighter than the liquid, the liquid can push it back above the surface. Then it floats.

18

Some boats are very big and very heavy. They can float because they have a lot of air inside.

All that air makes the boat lighter than the water in the ocean.

If you fill a metal pot with rocks, it will sink.

If people load too many things onto a boat, it can sink, too.

Vinegar   Maple syrup

Ping-Pong balls and plastic spoons don't just float in water. They can float in other liquids, too.

Maple syrup is a liquid that is heavier than water. It has more matter in the same amount of space. Some things that don't float on water can float on maple syrup.

An egg is too heavy to float in water. So it sinks!

But an egg can float in
maple syrup.

Did you know that
some liquids can float
on other liquids?

Water is lighter than maple
syrup. Water can float on
top of maple syrup.

Corn oil is lighter than
water. Corn oil can float
on top of water.

What else can float?
What else can sink?
Let's find out!

Words You Know

golf ball

maple syrup

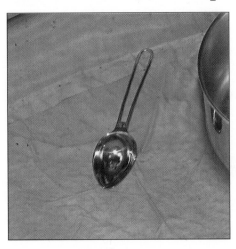

metal spoon

Ping-Pong ball

plastic spoon

Index

About the Author

Award-winning author Melissa Stewart has always been fascinated with the natural world and enjoys sharing it with others. She has written more than sixty science books for children.

Photo Credits